# I Love Crafts

# Cards
## and
# Wrapping Paper

HAVE A HUG!

Rita Storey

**PowerKiDS**
press

Published in 2017 by
**The Rosen Publishing Group, Inc.**
29 East 21st Street, New York, NY 10010

CATALOGING-IN-PUBLICATION DATA
Names: Storey, Rita.
Title: Cards and wrapping paper / Rita Storey.
Description: New York : PowerKids Press, 2017. | Series: I love crafts | Includes index.
Identifiers: ISBN 9781508150695 (pbk.) | ISBN 9781508150633 (library bound) |
ISBN 9781508150534 (6 pack)
Subjects: LCSH: Greeting cards--Juvenile literature. | Gift wraps--Juvenile literature. |
Paper work--Juvenile literature.
Classification: LCC TT872.S76 2017 | DDC 745.594'1--dc23

Designer: Rita Storey
Editor: Sarah Ridley
Crafts made by: Rita Storey
Series editor: Sarah Peutrill
Photography: Tudor Photography, Banbury
Cover images: Tudor Photography, Banbury

Manufactured in the United States of America
CPSIA Compliance Information: Batch #BS16PK:
For Further Information contact Rosen Publishing, New York, New York at 1-800-237-9932

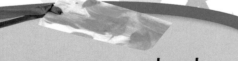

## Before you start

Some of the projects in this book require scissors, pins or a craft knife. When using these things we would recommend that children are supervised by a responsible adult.

**Please note:** Keep homemade cards away from babies and small children. They cannot be tested for safety.

## A Note About Measurements

Measurements are given in U.S. format with metric in parentheses. The metric conversion is rounded to make it easier to measure.

# Contents

# ★ Crazy Frame Card

Turn a picture of a cute animal or a pop star into a colorful card. Make it unique by decorating it with a collection of odds and ends from around the house.

## You will need:

* sheet of green card stock, 12 inch by 6 inch (30cm × 15cm)
* ruler  * pencil
* craft knife (ask an adult to use it)
* letter-sized sheet of yellow card stock
* glue and spreader
* picture or photo
* adhesive tape
* ribbon, patterned wrapping paper, feathers, buttons, stick-on craft jewels, candy wrappers

Opening

Fold

**1** Fold the card stock in half along the longest side. With the opening on the right, use the ruler to mark points 1⅛ inch (3cm) in from each corner. Draw lines, using the ruler, to join up the points to create a frame shape.

**2** Open out the card. Ask an adult to cut along the pencil lines with the craft knife as shown.

**3** Place the green card stock on top of the yellow card stock, matching up the corners. Draw along the inside of the frame using a pencil.

**4** Use the ruler to mark points 3/8 inch (1cm) out from the pencil lines. Draw lines, using the ruler, to join up the points and cut along these outer lines. This yellow card stock will form the backing for your picture.

**5** Cut out your picture. Glue it onto the yellow card stock.

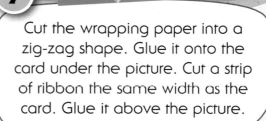

**7** Cut the wrapping paper into a zig-zag shape. Glue it onto the card under the picture. Cut a strip of ribbon the same width as the card. Glue it above the picture.

**6** Open the card. With the picture facing out through the frame, use adhesive tape to attach the yellow card stock to the green. Close the card.

**8** This card uses stickers, buttons, a candy wrapper, feathers and a piece of ribbon to finish it off. Decorate your card as you wish, using available materials.

# Monster Hug Card

This adorable monster has long fold-out arms to deliver a monster of a hug.

## You will need:

* pencil and 2 sheets of thin white paper (for tracing the templates)
* sewing pins
* fur fabric
* fabric scissors
* 11-inch-by-17-inch (28cm × 43cm) sheet of blue card stock
* fabric glue and spreader
* letter-sized sheet of yellow paper
* strip of yellow card stock, 24 inch by 1½ inch (60cm × 4cm)
* adhesive tape
* 2 googly eyes
* felt-tip pen

You could draw around your own hands instead of the hand template in step 5.

**1** Use thin white paper and a pencil to trace the body template on page 29. Cut it out and pin it onto the fur fabric. Cut out your fabric monster shape. Remove the pins and template and set to one side.

Fold

**2** Fold the blue card stock in half along the longest side. Place the top of the template on the fold. Draw around the template and cut it out.

**3** Open out the shape.

**4** Spread glue onto the smooth side of the fur monster. Glue it in place on the front of the card stock, matching the edges.

**5** Use thin white paper and a pencil to trace the hand template on page 29. Cut it out. Draw around the template on the yellow paper twice. Cut out two paper hands.

**6** Tape a paper hand to each end of the long strip of yellow paper.

**7** Tape the center of the long strip onto the back of the monster card.

**8** Glue the googly eyes onto the front of the monster card.

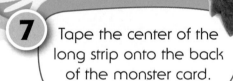

**9** Trace the speech bubble template on page 28 and cut out a blue card speech bubble. Write your own message and glue it in place.

HERE IS A BIG HUG FROM ME!

# Pop-up Ghost Card

This spooky card would make a great Halloween party invitation.

## You will need:

* two letter-sized sheets of thin purple card stock
* letter-sized sheet of yellow paper
* bowl, approx 6 inch (15cm) across
* pencil and thin white paper (for tracing the templates)
* scissors
* white glue and spreader
* letter-sized sheet of black card stock
* letter-sized sheet of white card stock
* black felt-tip pen
* stick-on stars

Once you have made this pop-up card, you could use the same skills to make cards for other occasions.

**1** Fold both sheets of purple card stock in half along the longest side.

**2** Draw around the bowl onto the yellow paper. Cut out the paper circle.

**3** Glue the paper circle onto the inside of one piece of folded card stock, as shown.

Fold

1½ inch (4cm)

1½ inch (4cm)

1½ inch (4cm)

**4** Use the pencil and thin white paper to trace the castle and bat templates on page 28. Place the templates on the black card stock and draw around them. Cut out the shapes.

**5** Glue the castle and bats in place, as shown.

**6** Fold the card shut. Use scissors to make two 1½-inch (4cm) cuts in the folded edge, 1½ inch (4cm) from the right-hand edge and 1½ inch (4cm) apart. Fold back the paper between the cuts. Crease the fold.

**7** Open out the card. Push the piece of card up between the cut lines. It should look like the picture above.

**8** Fold the card shut. Cover the outside of the card with a thin layer of glue. Put it inside the other sheet of folded purple card stock. Press flat and leave it to dry.

**9** Use the template on page 28 to cut out a ghost from the white card stock. Draw on eyes with the black felt-tip pen. Glue the ghost to the pop-up fold that sticks out, as shown. Stick on the stars (see main picture, right).

Write your message here.

9

# Stained Glass Card

This card looks good with light shining through it, just like a stained glass window. Place it near a window or a lamp to see it at its best.

## You will need:

* sheet of thick red paper, 12 inch by 6 inch (30cm × 15cm)

* sheet of thin black paper, 6 inch by 6 inch (15cm × 15cm)

* pencil and ruler

* scissors

* white glue and paintbrush

* clear plastic, 6 inch by 6 inch (15cm × 15cm), cut from a clear plastic folder for example

* masking tape

* torn-up pieces of colored tissue paper

Make an envelope out of a letter-sized piece of paper. See pages 26–27 for instructions.

**1** Fold the thick red paper in half along the longest side. Measure points $3/8$ inch (1cm) in from each corner and join them up to create a pencil line frame as shown in the picture above.

**2** Open the card and cut the middle section. Put the card to one side until you reach step 9.

**3** Fold the square of black paper in half from top to bottom.

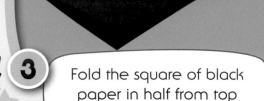

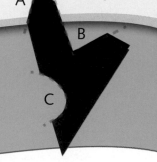

**4** Fold it in half again, as shown.

**5** Fold the paper again, from the folded corner to the corner diagonally opposite, as shown.

**6** Use scissors to cut off the top corner (A), as shown. Cut a triangular shape out of one side (B). Cut a semi-circular shape from the opposite side (C).

**7** Carefully unfold the paper to reveal the cut-out holes. Use pieces of masking tape to fix the square of plastic onto one side of the paper.

**8** Turn the paper over. Glue pieces of colored tissue to cover the cut-out holes. Leave everything to dry. Peel off the masking tape and plastic.

**9** Open the red card. Paste glue onto the inside of the paper frame. With the untidy side on the inside, press the decorated black paper in place. Leave it to dry.

**11**

# Rocket Card

Pull the tab for lift-off with this colorful moon rocket birthday card.

## You will need:

* black card stock, 8 inch by 8¼ inch (20cm × 21cm)
* letter-sized sheet of thin white paper
* letter-sized sheet of thin blue paper
* thick white paper, 3⅜ inch by 8¼ inch (8.5cm × 21cm)
* pencil
* scissors
* glue
* double-sided adhesive tape
* pink paper
* yellow paper
* red paper
* photograph of your friend that fits inside the center circle of the window
* fine black felt-tip pen
* stick-on craft jewels

**1** Fold the black card in half along the shorter side to create a tall card.

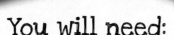

**2** Using the thin white paper and a pencil, trace the rocket template on page 29 and cut it out. Draw around the template on the blue paper. Cut it out.

**3** Open out the black card. Glue the rocket onto the front. Cut out the inside of the window. Ask an adult for help if you find this difficult.

**4** Stick a strip of double-sided tape to the inside of the long side of the card. Peel off the backing and close the card so that it sticks together.

**5** Trace the flame templates on page 29 onto thin white paper. Use the templates to cut out red and yellow paper flames. Stick them one on top of the other onto the thick white paper, 3/8 inch (1cm) from the bottom, as shown.

**6** With the flames facing up, slide the white paper inside the card. Leave 3/8 inch (1cm) of white paper showing at the bottom. Draw a circle inside the window.

**7** Gently, slide the white paper out of the card until the circle disappears. Draw another pencil circle inside the window.

HAPPY BIRTHDAY

**8** Slide the white paper out of the card. Cut out a picture of your friend to fit inside the top circle and glue it in place. Write a message in the lower circle.

**9** Trace the nose cone and window templates on page 29 onto thin white paper. Use the templates to cut out a pink window and a yellow nose cone. Glue them onto the card and stick the craft jewels around the window.

**10** Slide the strip of paper inside the card again, with the picture, the message and the flames facing up. The message will appear in the window. When you pull the paper tab, the picture will appear in the window.

# Sweet Flower Card

This flower has a sweet center and a butterfly you can eat. It is a card and a gift rolled into one.

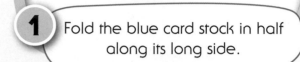

**1** Fold the blue card stock in half along its long side.

## You will need:

* thick blue card stock, 12 inch by 6 inch (30cm × 15cm)
* craft knife (ask an adult to use it)
* ruler  * scissors
* pen and thin white paper (for the template)
* yellow paper  * green paper
* pencil/compass
* red paper
* white glue and spreader
* lollipop
* double-sided adhesive tape
* pink paper
* wrapped piece of candy
* 2 googly eyes
* small orange pom-pom (from a craft shop)
* felt-tip pen

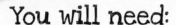

1½ inch (4cm)  ⅜ inch (1cm)  ¾ inch (2cm)

**2** Open up the card. Ask an adult to use the craft knife and the ruler to make two slits in the front of the card, as shown.

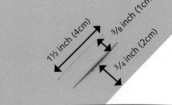

**3** Use the pen and thin white paper to trace the flower template on page 32. Cut it out and draw around it on the yellow paper. Cut out a yellow paper flower.

**4** Glue the yellow flower onto the card, just above the slits.

**5** Use the ruler to set the compass to ¾ inch (2cm). Now use the compass to draw a circle on the red paper. Cut it out.

**6** Glue the red circle onto the center of the yellow flower. Push the lollipop stick through the slit in the card, as shown.

**7** Trace the grass template on page 32. Use it to cut out green paper grass.

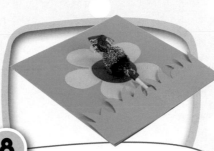

**8** Use double-sided tape to fix the paper grass in place, as shown, with the lollipop stick underneath the paper grass.

**9** Trace the butterfly wings template on page 32 and cut it out. Use it to cut out pink paper butterfly wings.

**10** Fold the paper wings in half and use double-sided tape to attach them to the wrapped candy, as shown. Glue the pom-pom to the candy.

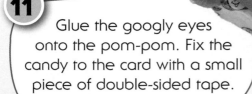

**11** Glue the googly eyes onto the pom-pom. Fix the candy to the card with a small piece of double-sided tape.

# Swimming Fish Card

These colorful fish are swimming in their own goldfish bowl. Send someone a birthday fish-wish!

## You will need:

* pencil and thin white paper (for tracing the template)
* scissors * white paper
* light blue card stock
* white glue and paintbrush
* small blue beads

AND

### For the goldfish:

* thick orange paper * 2 googly eyes
* two 6-inch (15cm) lengths of white embroidery thread
* adhesive tape

### For the patterned fish:

* thick patterned paper
* 2 googly eyes
* two 6-inch (15cm) lengths of white embroidery thread
* adhesive tape

**1** Use thin white paper and a pencil to trace the goldfish bowl template on pages 30–31. Cut it out. Draw around it on the light blue card stock.

**2** Cut along your pencil lines. Now your card should look like this.

**3** Spread some glue along the bottom of the card, as shown.

**4** Sprinkle on some blue beads and leave them to dry. Shake off any loose beads.

**5** Trace the water template on page 31 onto white paper and cut it out. Glue the paper water shape in place, as shown.

**6** Trace the fish template on page 31 and cut it out. Draw around the fish template on orange paper and cut it out. Fold across the fish tails and then open the paper out again.

**7** Brush glue onto one side of one fish and place the thread, as shown, onto the glue.

**8** Fold the other half over to trap the thread inside. Stick a googly eye on each side of the fish.

**9** Repeat steps 6–8 to make a second paper fish using patterned paper.

**10** Tape the threads to the top and bottom of the frame, as shown. Fold the card in half so that it can stand up.

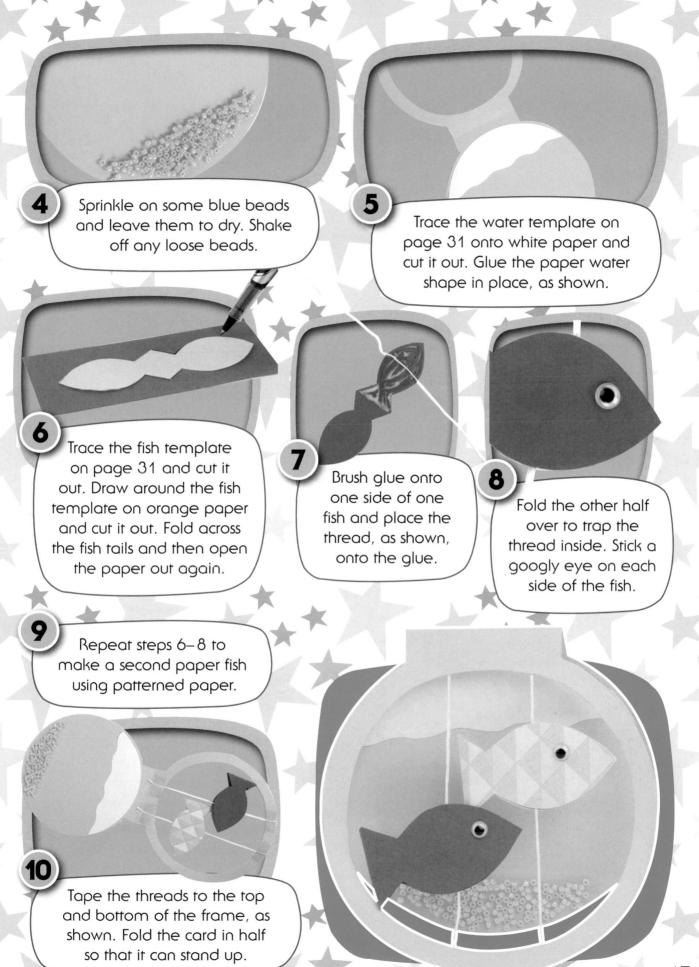

# Marbled Wrapping

This simple technique makes beautiful paper to wrap up small gifts and make them look special.

## You will need:

* shaving foam  * wooden spoon
* large baking tray or foil roasting dish
* bottles of yellow, blue, green, and red food coloring
* kitchen fork
* sheet of 11-inch by 17-inch (28cm × 43cm) paper for each print
* paper towel
* clothespins  * length of string tied between two points

**1**
Use the wooden spoon to spread a thin layer of shaving foam across the bottom of a baking tray.

**2**
Drop dots of food coloring onto the surface of the shaving foam. Use the fork to create swirling patterns of color.

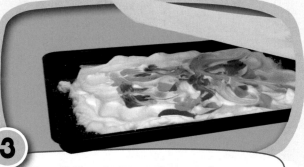

**3**
Carefully place a sheet of paper on top of the shaving foam.

**4**
Gently smooth the paper down so that it picks up the swirling colors.

**5** Carefully lift off the paper. Wipe away any extra shaving foam with a piece of paper towel.

**6** Hang your sheet of marbled paper up to dry using a clothespin.

**7** Repeat steps 3–6 to get a similar piece of wrapping paper or mix the colors up for a change. Add another color or start again, to make a completely different pattern.

**8** If you use white card stock instead of paper, you can make cards and gift tags to match your wrapping paper.

# Printed Wrapping

**W**rap gifts in style with your own printed wrapping paper.

## You will need:

* medium-sized uncooked potato
* kitchen knife (ask an adult to use it)
* paper towel

### For the heart print paper:

* green felt-tip pen
* red paint
* paintbrush
* large sheet of brown parcel paper

### For the elephant print paper:

* fine tip black felt-tip pen
* pink paint
* paintbrush
* large sheet of white paper

If you would like to make Christmas wrapping paper, cut your wedge of potato into the shape of a Christmas tree or a star.

## Potato print hearts

**1** Ask an adult to cut a ¾-inch (2cm) wedge from a potato. Dry one side of the potato with paper towel. Draw a simple heart shape onto it.

**2** Ask an adult to use a kitchen knife to cut around the heart shape.

**3** Dab red paint on one side of the potato heart.

# Potato print elephants

**4** Press the potato heart onto the brown paper. Lift it off. Move it down and print again. When the prints get faint, add more paint. When you are happy with your design, leave it to dry.

**1** Ask an adult to cut a ¾-inch (2cm) wedge from a potato. Dry one side of the potato with paper towel. Use the template on page 32 or copy the elephant shape shown here onto the potato.

**2** Ask an adult to use a kitchen knife to cut around the elephant shape.

**3** Dab pink paint on one side of the potato elephant.

**4** Press the potato elephant onto the white paper. Lift it off. Move it to a different position and print again. When the prints get faint, add more paint. Leave the printed paper to dry.

**5** Use the black felt-tip pen to draw an eye, an ear, a tail, and toes, copying the picture shown here. Repeat for each elephant.

## You will need:

### For the flower print paper:

* wire scouring pads
* large sheet of white paper
* red paint  * saucer  * pink paint
* green felt-tip pen

### For the fingerprint chicks paper:

* yellow paint  * saucer  * scrap paper
* large sheet of white paper
* fine tip black felt-tip pen

### For crazy stripes paper:

* square of corrugated cardboard
* yellow paint  * bright pink paint
* paintbrush
* large sheet of white paper

## Flower print paper

**1** Dip the end of the scouring pad into the saucer of red paint. Print it onto the paper. Repeat, leaving spaces between the prints, as shown on the finished wrapping paper.

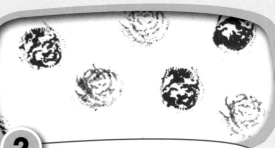

**2** Fill in the spaces in your design by making pink rose prints, following the instructions in step 1.

**3** Use the felt-tip pen to draw a stem and a leaf, as shown here, to complete each flower.

# Fingerprint chicks paper

**1** Dip your finger in the saucer of yellow paint.

**2** Press your finger onto a sheet of scrap paper to remove any excess paint.

**3** Make a fingerprint on the large sheet of paper. Repeat steps 1 to 3 until your wrapping paper is covered with yellow fingerprints. Leave to dry.

**4** Draw wings, feathers, legs and feet onto each chick, as shown here.

# Crazy stripes paper

**1** Brush yellow paint onto the corrugated cardboard. Press it onto the paper. Repeat until the paper is covered with stripes. Leave to dry.

**2** Brush bright pink paint onto the corrugated cardboard. Press it onto the paper. Repeat to make a random pattern.

# Party Bags

Make several of these decorated bags to use as party bags at your next birthday party, or use one instead of wrapping paper.

## To make a bag you will need:

* pencil and thin white paper (for tracing the template)

* scissors

* masking tape

* double-sided adhesive tape

AND

### For the Superhero bag:

* letter-sized sheet of orange paper

* blue paper

* yellow paper

* silver stars

### For the princess bag:

* letter-sized sheet of green paper

* pink paper  * yellow paper

* stick-on craft jewels

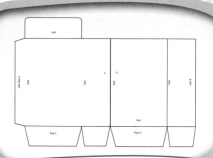

**1** Use thin white paper and a pencil to trace the party bag templates on pages 30–31. Cut them out. Tape them together along the sides marked X.

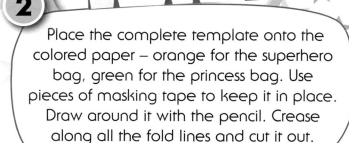

**2** Place the complete template onto the colored paper – orange for the superhero bag, green for the princess bag. Use pieces of masking tape to keep it in place. Draw around it with the pencil. Crease along all the fold lines and cut it out.

**3** Take off the masking tape and the template. It should look like this.

**4** Stick a strip of double-sided tape onto side flap A. Peel off the backing. Tape it onto side B.

**5** Stick a strip of double-sided tape onto flap C. Peel off the backing.

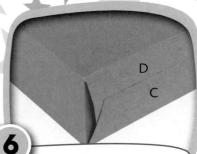

**6** Fold the flap up and stick it onto flap D.

**7** Press in the sides along the creases. Fold down the top flap.

## Superhero

**1** Trace the lightning flash templates on page 31. Use the bigger one to cut out a blue flash and the smaller one to cut out a yellow flash. Glue the blue one onto an orange gift bag.

**2** Glue the yellow flash onto the center of the blue one, as shown. Stick on silver stars.

## Princess

**1** Trace and cut out the crown templates on page 31. Use them to cut out one pink and one yellow crown. Glue the pink crown onto the green gift bag.

**2** Glue the yellow crown onto the center of the pink crown. Add stick-on jewels.

# Make an Envelope

An envelope is a lovely finishing touch to your homemade card. This way of making an envelope will work with all of the cards in this book.

## You will need:

* a piece of paper: it needs to measure the same as the height of your card plus 3 inches (8cm) and twice the width of your card plus 2¼ inches (6cm)

* card stock   * glue   * scissors
* ruler   * pencil

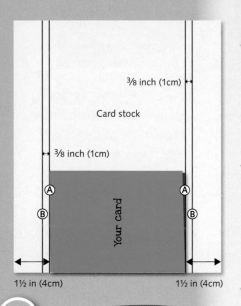

³/8 inch (1cm)

Card stock

³/8 inch (1cm)

Ⓐ   Ⓐ

Ⓑ   Ⓑ

Your card

1½ in (4cm)   1½ in (4cm)

**1**
Start by placing your card on the base of the card stock, 1½ inches (4cm) from the left-hand edge.

Draw lines on the card stock along the sides of your card. Extend the lines across the card stock (**A**).

Now draw parallel lines ³/8 inch (1cm) from each side of the card. Extend these lines the entire length of the card stock (**B**).

Card stock

³/8 inch (1cm)

³/8 inch (1cm)

Ⓒ Ⓓ Ⓔ

Your card

**2**
Draw a line across the card stock along the top edge of your card (**C**).

Draw a parallel line ³/8 inch (1cm) above the card (**D**).

Draw a parallel line ³/4 inch (2cm) above your card (**E**).

1½ in (4cm)

³/8 inch (1cm)

Ⓕ Ⓖ

Your card

Ⓔ

**3**
Place your card on line **E**.

Draw a line along the top edge of your card (**F**).

Draw a parallel line ³/8 inch (1cm) above the top of the card (**G**).

Your card

1½ in (4cm)

Ⓕ Ⓖ ⬍ ³⁄₈ inch (1cm)

Ⓗ                                                    Ⓗ

Ⓔ ⬍ ³⁄₈ inch (1cm)
Ⓒ Ⓓ                          ⬍ ³⁄₈ inch (1cm)

Ⓐ                                              Ⓐ
Ⓑ                                              Ⓑ

↞ ³⁄₈ inch (1cm)            ³⁄₈ inch (1cm) ↠

1½ in (4cm)                                1½ in (4cm)

**4** Join up the lines shown in pink. Cut the shapes out of the card stock.

**5** Fold the paper along lines **B**, **D**, and **G**.

**6** Fold the side flaps in. Glue flaps at the top of the card stock (**H**) to the outside of the envelope.

**7** Pop your card into the envelope and glue the top flap down or tuck the flap inside the envelope.

# Templates

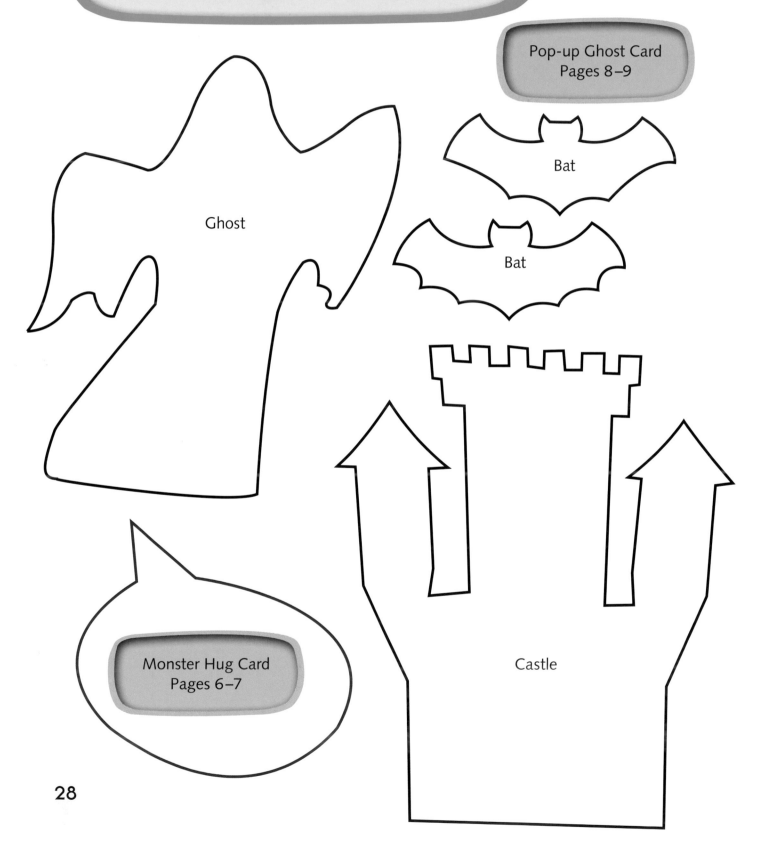

Pop-up Ghost Card
Pages 8–9

Ghost

Bat

Bat

Castle

Monster Hug Card
Pages 6–7

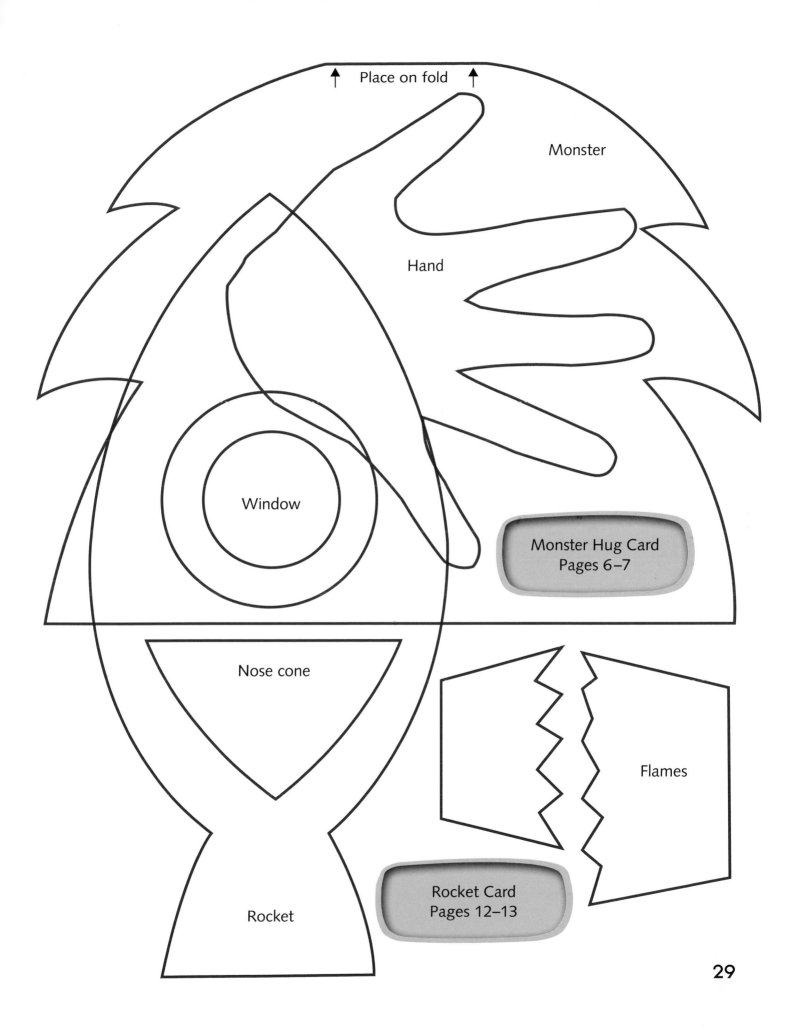

Place on fold

Monster

Hand

Window

Monster Hug Card
Pages 6–7

Nose cone

Flames

Rocket Card
Pages 12–13

Rocket

29

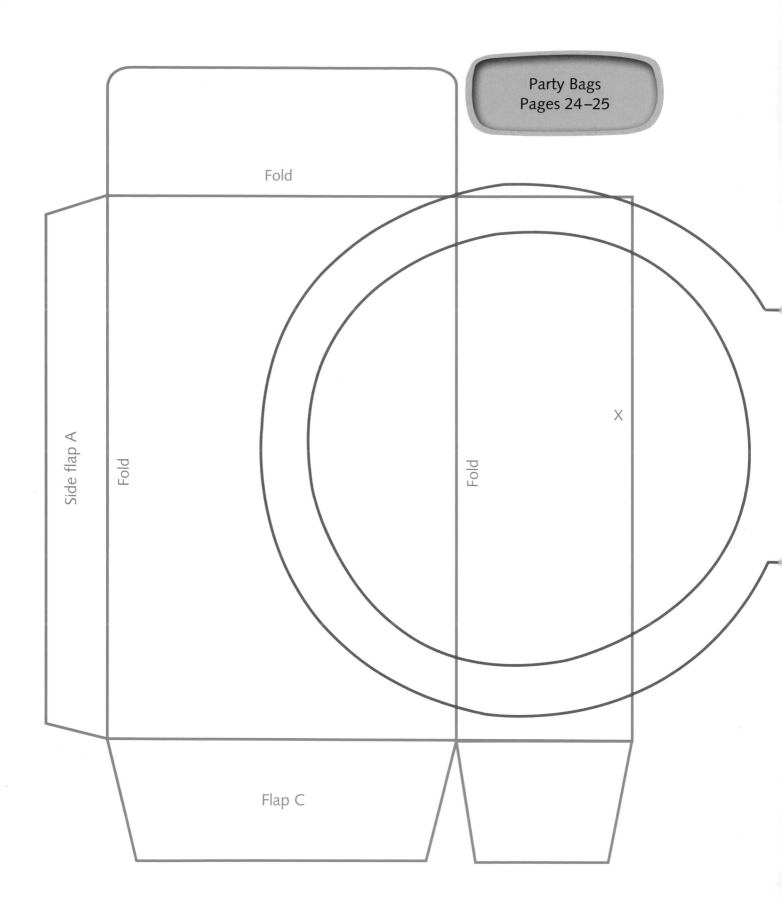

Fold

Party Bags
Pages 24–25

Side flap A

Fold

Fold

X

Flap C